4 1974 10173 600 4

HIST⊘RY

SERIES TITLES

15, 16-17, 18, 24-25, 30-31, 32-33, 34-35, 39; Paola Ravaglia p. 12; Andrea Ricciardi di Gaudesi pp. 22-23; Sergio pp. 40-41.

Other illustrations: Studio Stalio (Alessandro Cantucci, Fabiano Fabbrucci, Margherita Salvadori)

Maps: Paola Baldanzi

Photography: Bridgeman Art Library, London/Alinari Photo Library, Firenze pp. 9t, 29br, 44-45bc; Scala Archives, Firenze pp. 7tc, 20b, 27b, 37tc.

Art Director: Marco Nardi

Layouts: Starry Dogs Books Ltd.

Project Editor: Loredana Agosta

Research: Claire Moore, Ellie Smith

Editing: Tall Tree Ltd, London

Repro: Litocolor, Florence

Consultant:

Dr. Joseph Bergin is Professor of Modern History at Manchester University and Fellow of the British Academy. His research interests are mainly in the religious, social and political history of early modern France from the later sixteenth to the eighteenth century.

Library of Congress Cataloging-in-Publication Data

Malam, John, 1957-
  The birth of modern nations / John Malam.
      p. cm. -- (History of the world ; 12)
  Includes index.
  Summary: "A detailed overview of the history of Europe from about 1600 to 1700, during which modern nations came into power"--Provided by publisher.
  ISBN 978-8860981554
  1. Europe--History--17th century--Juvenile literature. I. Title.
  D246.M27 2009
  940.2'3--dc22
                                        2008008570

Printed and bound in Malaysia.

THE BIRTH OF MODERN NATIONS
was created and produced by McRae Books Srl
Via del Salviatino, 1 — 50016 — Fiesole (Florence), (Italy)
info@mcraebooks.com
www.mcraebooks.com

Publishers: Anne McRae, Marco Nardi
Series Editor: Anne McRae
Author: John Malam
Main Illustrations: Giacinto Gaudenzi pp. 42-43; MM comunicazione (Manuela Cappon, Monica Favilli) pp. 10,

HISTORY

Birth of Modern Nations

John Malam

Consultant: Dr. Joseph Bergin, Professor of Modern History at Manchester University, Fellow of the British Academy.

Zak BOOKS

Contents

The Battle of the White Mountain (near Prague) in 1620 was one of the major clashes of the Thirty Years' War. The imperial Habsburg army routed the disorganised Bohemian forces of Frederick V (reigned 1619–1620).

TIMELINE

	1600 CE	1620	1630	1640
HOLY ROMAN EMPIRE		Start of the Thirty Years' War.	Swedish troops enter Germany.	Emperor Leopold I succeeds Ferdinand III. — Treaty of Westphalia.
BRITAIN	James VI of Scotland becomes James I of England. — Parliament dissolved.	Death of James I.		Bishops' Wars in Scotland. — Civil war begins in England.
FRANCE	King Henri IV of France is assassinated.	Cardinal Richelieu becomes chief minister in France.		Death of King Louis XIII.
SPAIN AND PORTUGAL	Reign of Philip III over Spain and Portugal.	Spain enters the Thirty Years' War.		Portugal regains independence. João IV becomes king of Portugal.
THE NETHERLANDS	Truce with Spain establishes an independent republic in the Netherlands.			Spain finally acknowledges Dutch independence.
ITALIAN STATES	Venice rejects papal authority in secular government.		Scientist Galileo Galilei is placed under house arrest by the Church.	Revolt in Naples.
SCANDINAVIA AND EASTERN EUROPE	Bethlen Gábor invades Hungary.	Gustavus Adolphus of Sweden creates Europe's first modern army.		

Introduction

The time from the late 16th century to the start of the 18th century is referred to as the Early Modern Period because it witnessed the emergence of countries and institutions that survive to this day. The Netherlands and Portugal won their independence, England and Scotland were united to form Great Britain, and Russia emerged as a world power. By contrast, the vast and widely scattered Holy Roman Empire, which had dominated politics in the Medieval period, began its long decline. There was a continuing struggle between absolute monarchy and the rising power of people's representative assemblies, such as parliaments. International trade and overseas empires developed, as did new systems of commerce. Scientists made major advances, and cities grew as more people moved from the countryside.

This is the royal standard of King Charles I of England (reigned 1625–1649). When Charles dissolved Parliament in his quest for absolute power, civil war broke out.

Seventeenth-century executions could be unusually brutal. The assassin who killed King Henri IV of France (reigned 1594–1610) was torn apart for his crime.

1650	1660	1670	1680	1690

Oliver Cromwell crushes Catholic rebellion in Ireland.

Charles II proclaimed king of Scots in Edinburgh.

The Fronde of the Princes ends in victory for Mazarin and absolute monarchy.

Spain regains Catalonia.

Velázquez paints *Las Meniñas*.

Abdication of Queen Christina of Sweden.

The Russians capture Vilnius.

Restoration of the monarchy.

Treaty of alliance between Spain and England.

France invades Spanish Netherlands (now Belgium).

Siege of Copenhagen.

Modern boundaries of Denmark, Sweden and Norway are established.

Cosimo III becomes grand duke of Tuscany. Period of decline in Tuscany begins.

Jan III Sobieski becomes king of Poland.

Revocation of the Edict of Nantes.

Reign of King Pedro II of Portugal.

William III, prince of Orange, becomes king of England.

France gains control of Genoa from Spain.

Pope Innocent XI organises Holy League against the Ottoman Turks.

Bank of England founded.

The death of Queen Elizabeth I (reigned 1558–1603) opened the way for peace with Spain and increased trade.

Europe in 1600

For most Europeans life in 1600 was a struggle against many hardships. People were still at the mercy of the weather, which might bring famine or plenty. Conflicts continued, although their causes were changing, with fewer wars of religion but more political rebellions. Trade was growing, bringing in new kinds of food and luxuries such as tobacco. Spain and Portugal had won empires overseas, and other European countries would soon follow.

The European Economy

The growth in world trade favored new, seagoing powers such as the Dutch and the English. Trade and banking flourished: companies were founded to trade in Asia, and the Amsterdam Exchange Bank opened in 1609. As prosperity grew, so did the population, especially in towns—for example, London's rose from 200,000 people (1600) to 500,000 (1700). A higher demand for food made farming more productive.

These women are making silk, one of Europe's boom industries of the time. Lyon in France was a major center for the trade.

Ruling Powers

The richest, most powerful European country in 1600 was still Spain, but France would soon overtake it. Later in the 17th century a new power emerged—Russia, which had had little contact with western Europe until Peter the Great (reigned 1682–1725) became tsar. Signs of Prussia's future greatness appeared after 1640. Abroad, the French and English founded colonies in North America, while the Dutch explored the Pacific.

France's institutions were highly developed. These magistrates of the Parlement de Paris, the most prestigious higher court of law in France, sat in the Palais de Justice.

EUROPE IN 1600

Population Density
The population centres of Europe in about 1600 were always close to a coast or navigable river. The areas of high population were similar to today's, with Italy, France and the Low Countries the most densely populated.

- Highest population
- Fairly high population
- Average population
- Low population

The Calling of St. Peter *by Caravaggio, who was a master of painting light and shade. Daring and highly expressive, he used ordinary people as his models.*

Art

The main style in art and architecture of the 17th century is called Baroque, which was expressed in many different forms and often had little in common with the Baroque in Italy, where it started. Italian influence in the arts was no longer so strong, although the innovative Michelangelo Caravaggio (1571–1610) revived Baroque art in Rome. Other great artists of the age were the Flemish Peter Paul Rubens (1577–1640), Nicholas Poussin (1594–1665) of France, and the Dutch painter, Rembrandt (1606–1669).

Music and Literature

There were great advances in music, with the Italian Claudio Monteverdi (1567–1643) writing the first ever opera. In France, Pierre Corneille (1606–1684) and Jean Racine (1639–1699) wrote superb classical dramas, while Molière (1622–1673) produced comedies. English literature was flourishing, too—William Shakespeare (1564–1616) was perhaps Europe's best playwright. He died the same year as brilliant Spanish novelist Miguel de Cervantes (1547–1616).

Shakespeare's plays were first performed in London's Globe Theatre.

The Habsburg Empire

A continuing theme of European history was the competition among ruling dynasties to increase their lands and wealth. The most successful were the Habsburgs, a royal German family who became powerful when Rudolf I (reigned 1273–1291) was elected king. The Habsburgs also ruled Hungary and Bohemia, and Spain. Their empire reached its height in the 16th century with the reign of Charles V. After his death the dynasty was split into two: the Spanish and the Austrian lines. Habsburg rule lasted until Austria's defeat in the First World War (1918).

The Habsburg Failure

The Habsburg central government needed reform, such as making the imperial Diet (containing the princes' representatives) into a parliament that could make laws for the whole empire. The difficulty was that the German princes preferred to keep the emperor's authority at arm's length, and so resisted any reform that strengthened his position.

This silver goblet made in 1645 features the portraits of each Habsburg emperor from Charles V to Ferdinand II.

The 17th-century crown of the Holy Roman Emperors.

The Holy Roman Emperor

This title of the Habsburg rulers was meant to recall the ancient Roman empire, and it was "Holy" because it was Christian. As protector of the Church and an ally of the Pope, the emperor was supposed to be above other rulers. But the many states in the empire had their own rulers, among them the various princes who elected the emperor.

A medallion belonging to Anne of Austria (1601–66), daughter of Philip III of Spain. She is shown with her son, the future Louis XIV of France (see pages 22–23).

THE HABSBURG EMPIRE 1556–1618

Spanish Habsburgs

Austrian Habsburgs

Permanent allies of the Habsburgs

Boundary of the Holy Roman Empire in 1618

NORTH SEA
BALTIC SEA
ENGLAND
UNITED PROVINCES
BRANDENBURG
POLAND-LITHUANIA
SPANISH NETHERLANDS
BOHEMIA
FRANCE
ATLANTIC OCEAN
FRANCHE COMTE
VIENNA
AUSTRIA
HUNGARY
MILAN
GENOA
OTTOMAN EMPIRE
PORTUGAL
FLORENCE
MADRID
CORSICA
SPAIN
NAPLES
SARDINIA
MEDITERRANEAN SEA
SICILY

Habsburg Territories

The largest empire was held by Charles V, who was already ruler of Spain and other countries when elected Holy Roman Emperor in 1519. In theory, Charles V controlled half of Europe, but each territory had its own separate government, and he had many enemies, including the Ottoman Empire, France and others who feared Habsburg power. Although vast, Charles' empire was only a personal one. He could never combine his many lands into one. In the end he abdicated, worn out, in 1556, leaving the Spanish crown to his son Philip II, and the empire to his brother Ferdinand I. The Spanish line ended when the last Habsburg king died in 1700.

Archduke Albert Ernst of Austria (1559–1621) and his wife, Isabella Clara Eugenia (1566–1633), daughter of Philip II of Spain, visit a so-called collector's cabinet. This was a room displaying all kinds of rare objects and curiosities, rather like a small private museum.

The Emperor Ferdinand II invited missionaries from Rome to Vienna to combat Protestantism. Their church builders introduced the Roman Baroque style, which strongly influenced architecture in late 17th-century Vienna. The Church of St Charles in Vienna (left) was completed in 1715.

The Habsburgs and the Dutch

The Low Countries (roughly, modern Belgium and Holland) came into Habsburg possession in 1477. Protestantism was strong in this part of Europe, and the efforts of Philip II to destroy it resulted in the Revolt of the Netherlands in 1566. The Union of Utrecht (1579) divided the United Provinces (the northern Netherlands), which demanded independence, from the Spanish (southern) Netherlands. A truce ended the war in 1609, but Spain did not recognize Dutch independence until 1648.

Religious Division

After the Reformation, many states of the empire were Protestant, which the emperors, as protectors of the Roman Church, resisted. Emperors such as Rudolf II and Ferdinand II were devout Catholics, and their fierce attacks on Protestantism were one of the causes of the outbreak of the Thirty Years' War in 1618. War ended any hopes of imperial reform—the empire remained a loose association of more than 300 independent principalities.

The Thirty Years' War

Someone born in Germany in 1618 would have been 30 before they knew peace. The Thirty Years' War was long and destructive. It involved most of the countries of Europe, and it changed the balance of power among them. On one side, the Habsburg emperor combined with the Habsburg king of Spain. Their various opponents included France, which by 1648 had become the most powerful European nation.

This print shows the incident called the Defenestration ("throwing out of a window") of Prague, which sparked the Thirty Years' War.

Most armies used muskets like this. They were slow and unreliable, but a musket ball, unlike an arrow, could pierce steel armour at 330 feet (100 m).

Origins of the War

It began as a religious war. The Protestants of Prague, the Bohemian capital, resented their treatment by the Catholic authorities. When the Catholic Emperor Ferdinand II ignored their complaints, they threw his governors out of a window and a rising began. A Protestant prince, Frederick, was elected king, but the Protestants were divided, and Ferdinand defeated them at the Battle of the White Mountain in 1620. That might have ended the matter, but others were drawn in and the civil war became a continental conflict.

Weapons and Armour

Although most soldiers still wore a helmet and a breastplate, in an age of gunpowder weapons body armor became increasingly ineffective. The fighting was often confused and messy, mainly because of the problems caused by the mixture of muskets and pikes among the infantry. Swedish field artillery, using smallish guns organised in groups, was especially effective.

The Opposing Sides

German Protestant states, alarmed at Ferdinand's early success in the war, persuaded the Protestant king of Denmark, Christian IV (reigned 1596–1648), to help them. Christian hoped to win German land but, after some victories, he was soon defeated. Habsburg armies raged across northern Germany, killing thousands of Protestant civilians. Meanwhile, another Protestant king, Gustavus II of Sweden (reigned 1611–1632), entered the war. A military genius, he was never defeated, but died during his last victory.

A suit of armor used by Protestant arquebusiers (gunmen) in about 1620.

Peace at Last

Peace treaties ending the Thirty Years' War were signed at several cities in the Westphalia region of Saxony, although France and Spain did not make peace until the Treaty of the Pyrenees (1659). The Westphalia settlement made the German states practically independent of the emperor's authority, and gave equality to Catholics and Protestants. It confirmed the power of Sweden, France, and the independent Dutch republic, and the decline of Spain.

Gustavus II of Sweden was usually known as Gustavus Adolphus. He was a brilliant general who led the finest army of the day.

A souvenir of the Treaty of Westphalia in 1648—a German beer mug decorated with figures of the peacemakers.

The Habsburg Defeat

Gustavus had financial support from France, which, although a Catholic country was a bitter rival of the Habsburgs. By the time France declared war in 1635, religion was no longer a significant issue in the fighting. Allied with the Swedes and some Protestant German states, the French won victories at Rocroi against the Spanish (1643), and at Freiburg (1644) and Nördlingen (1645) against the Bavarians and Austrians. But the emperor refused to give in until further defeats left him with no choice.

At the Battle of Breitenfeld in 1631, the Swedish won the first major Protestant victory against the Catholic imperial forces.

THE THIRTY YEARS' WAR

1618 Defenestration of Prague.

1620 Battle of the White Mountain near Prague.

1624 Cardinal Richelieu becomes chief minister in France.

1630 Swedish troops enter Germany.

1631 Protestant citizens of Magdeburg massacred.

1632 Gustavus Adolphus defeats Habsburg army at the River Lech.

1632 Swedish victory at Lützen; Gustavus Adolphus killed.

1635 France allies with Sweden against the Habsburgs.

1648 Treaty of Westphalia.

der Abentewerlich Simplicissimus Teütsch

The humorous Adventures of a Simpleton (this is its front cover) describes some of the horrors of the Thirty Years' War. It was written by the German Hans Jakob von Grimmelshausen (1621–1676), who fought in the war.

Mercenary soldiers caused much destruction, but after the war many were left impoverished, wounded and disease-ridden.

After the Thirty Years' War

War usually slowed economic development, but it also speeded up trends that were already under way. For example, the Baltic region's Hanseatic League of trading cities disappeared at the end of the war, but this commercial network was already failing in 1618. Although Germany seemed devastated by the fighting, damage was regional and so recovery was quick. Hamburg, which suffered little damage, prospered: its population grew by 35 percent. Magdeburg, brutally sacked in 1631, was completely rebuilt by 1680.

Effects of War

Some parts of Germany were a wilderness at the end of the war, with ruined buildings, few people and no livelihood. The peasants suffered most, and some villages were abandoned altogether. Population losses can only be guessed, but probably 5–10 million people died. Fighting and violence by marauding soldiers were not the chief killers. Disease caused more deaths, especially among children. Other, political effects appeared later. The reduced power of the emperor gave increased power to the German princes, and some won more land.

The Siege of Vienna began in early July 1683. When Sobieski's army arrived in August, the Turks had already mined under the walls.

17TH CENTURY

1618
Elector of Brandenburg inherits Duchy of Prussia.

1637
Emperor Ferdinand III succeeds Ferdinand II.

1653
The Great Elector abolishes the estates (representative assemblies).

1656
Swedes surrender part of Pomerania to Great Elector.

1674
Jan III Sobieski becomes king of Poland.

1684
French Huguenots offered refuge in Brandenburg.

1688
Frederick III succeeds the Great Elector in Brandenburg.

1697
Eugene of Savoy, an Austrian general, defeats the Turks at Zenta.

1701
Frederick III of Brandenburg crowned as King Frederick I of Prussia.

The Siege of Vienna

In 1683, Emperor Leopold I called for help against a huge Turkish force attacking Vienna. A few German states responded, as did Jan III Sobieski, king of Poland (reigned 1674–1696). Jan assembled an army and marched 500 km (300 mi) from Crakow to Vienna. The Turks outnumbered his forces by three to one, but he wore them down with artillery fire. When Jan's cavalry attacked at the ideal moment, the Turks fled.

Portrait of Frederick William, known as the Great Elector.

The Great Elector

In the late 17th century, Prussia was developing from a fairly minor princedom—he electorate of Brandenburg— into the efficient military state that would one day unite Germany under its leadership. Brandenburg had suffered badly during the Thirty Years' War, but Frederick William, the "Great Elector" (reigned 1640–1688), made it the greatest German state after Austria. He created a powerful army, won influence and territory by skilful diplomacy and limited warfare, centralized the government, and reformed the economy to make Brandenburg prosperous.

Perhaps Leopold I's greatest virtue was his strong sense of duty. He succeeded Ferdinand III as emperor in 1657 and died in 1705—a reign of nearly 50 years.

Leopold's architect for the palace of Schönbrunn, Vienna, was the famous Fischer von Erlach (1656–1723). In 1700, it had domes, which have since been demolished.

Emperor Leopold I

Leopold I was less powerful than his predecessors, and, given the problems he faced, had no wish to expand the Habsburg empire. The Turks continued to attack his borders and he faced the aggressive policies of Louis XIV of France (reigned 1643–1715). A central figure in anti-French alliances, Leopold created a permanent army, reformed central government, and regained Hungary from the Turks—but lost Strasbourg to France.

1567
James inherits Scottish crown at 13 months old.

1585
James begins to rule in Scotland.

1603
James VI of Scotland becomes James I of England.

1607
First colonists settle in Jamestown, Virginia.

1609
"Plantation" of Ulster with Scots and English.

1614
"Addled Parliament" is dismissed by James without passing laws.

1616
Death of Shakespeare.

1625
Death of James I.

Union of Crowns

Although James was king of both Scotland and England, they kept separate governments. James was clever, but had little common sense; in some ways he made a poor king. Yet he believed he was appointed to rule by God. He was very annoyed when his policies were attacked by his parliaments or by religious Puritans who thought the English Church too Catholic.

James I was physically weak. He sometimes had to be tied to his horse, and dribbled when he talked.

IRELAND IN THE 17TH CENTURY

ATLANTIC OCEAN

DUNLUCE
COLERAINE
LONDONDERRY
COUNTY ANTRIM
UFFORD STRABANE
CARRICKFERGUS
BANGOR
DONEGAL
BELFAST
NEWTOWNARDS
DUNGANNON
ENNISKILLEN
COUNTY DOWN
NEWRY
IRISH SEA

The "Plantation" of Ulster

Because of the difficulties of governing rebellious Irish Catholics, the English government decided to "plant" colonies of Scottish and English Protestants in Ulster, the most difficult province. Irish land was confiscated and given to the settlers, Irish culture was almost destroyed, and the old Irish aristocracy disappeared. Some land was also given to the Church and to Trinity College, Dublin. The counties of Antrim and Down were excluded because much "plantation" had already happened there privately.

- English settlers
- Trinity College and the Church
- Londonderry plantation
- Scottish settlers
- Irish
- Private plantations

Arguments over Religion

There were fierce religious differences in England. The English Anglican Church suited James and the bishops, but Puritans wanted a stricter religion. The problem was debated at Hampton Court, near London, in 1604. Nothing was decided, but a new Bible translation was ordered–the famous King James Bible.

Britain under James I

Queen Elizabeth I of England had no children. The question of who would succeed her worried her ministers. The heir had to have a claim to the crown by birth, but must also be a Protestant. James VI, king of Scotland, was a descendant Elizabeth's grandfather, and an admirer of the English Church, so England's ministers agreed that James should inherit the throne.

While at sea on the Mayflower, *the Pilgrim Fathers drew up the "Mayflower Compact," which was a plan of government for their new colony.*

Here are some designs (never used) for a flag combining the English Cross of St George with the Scottish Saltire of St. Andrew.

The Mayflower

Among the groups fleeing religious persecution in the early 17th century were those we know as the Pilgrim Fathers. They disliked the English Church so much they moved to the Netherlands. Later, deciding to start a new life overseas, they sailed in the *Mayflower* from Plymouth in 1620 and founded "New Plymouth" in Massachusetts. Apart from a few settlers in Virginia, they were the first English colonists in North America.

In 1605, Guy Fawkes was caught placing gunpowder in the cellars of the English Parliament, an act provoked by the English refusal to give Catholics better treatment.

The Gunpowder Plot

A group of rebellious Catholics, whose church was illegal in England, planned to blow up king and Parliament on 5 November 1605. The plot was discovered a day earlier, and the conspirators executed after torture. It increased the fear and hatred of Catholicism among English Protestants who treated Catholics as traitors.

Most famous of Inigo Jones' surviving buildings are the Banqueting House in Whitehall, London (shown here), and the Queen's House in Greenwich.

Architecture

The first professional architect and designer in England was Inigo Jones (1573–1652). He understood the principles of the art of the Italian Renaissance, and had studied in Italy, especially the works of Andrea Palladio (1508–1580), after whom the style Palladian is named. As Surveyor of the King's Works, Inigo Jones also designed settings for court entertainments.

Birth of the Commonwealth

Like his father, James I, Charles I of England believed in the divine right of kings. His attempt to rule as an absolute monarch led to bitter quarrels with Parliament, which in 1642 spiralled into civil war. Fighting devastated much of Britain and resulted in Charles' execution and the establishment of an English Commonwealth under Oliver Cromwell.

Charles I was a wise patron of the arts. He employed the skilful Dutch painter Van Dyck (1599–1641), whose portraits of him, as here, made him look very regal.

Charles I

From 1629, Charles ruled without Parliament. However, he had to recall it in 1640 in order to raise the money needed to crush the Scottish "Bishops' Wars," which were caused by his efforts to force Anglican worship on the Presbyterian Scots. Parliament would not vote any taxes until the king first accepted its demands. Charles refused, but Parliament's hostility won him many supporters. Now a strong royalist party existed. Charles could raise an army, and in 1642 civil war broke out.

The Civil War in England

At first no-one expected Parliament to win, and no-one could imagine what would happen if it did. But Parliament controlled the navy, blocking Royalist reinforcements from abroad, and, most important, it controlled London, the center of both wealth and power. The Royalists, with the best cavalry, did well at first, but Parliament, with Scottish assistance, won the decisive battle of Marston Moor in 1644. Next year, Charles' forces were smashed by Cromwell's "New Model Army" at Naseby.

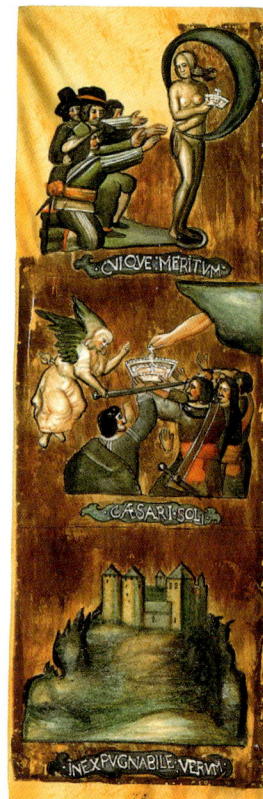

Royalist cavalry flags were later made into this decorative panel. Charles' best general was Prince Rupert of the Rhine (1619–1682), his cousin.

The soldiers of the Royalist army receive their wages at the camp. Inability to pay soldiers their wages was a serious problem. Some went for months without pay.

CIVIL WAR IN ENGLAND AND WALES

EDINBURGH • DUNBAR
GLASGOW
BELFAST • NEWCASTLE
MARSTON
MOOR • HULL
DUBLIN LIVERPOOL SHEFFIELD
WEXFORD NEWARK
WORCESTER • NASEBY
OXFORD LONDON
BRISTOL SOUTHAMPTON
TORBAY

Areas controlled by Parliament in 1642

Areas controlled by Charles I in 1645

A Land Divided
Charles gained support from some parts of the kingdom but he was no match for Parliament, which took control of the major ports, including London, Bristol, and Hull. He lost control of northern England thanks to the Scots, who sided with Parliament. By 1651, the Royalist forces were decisively beaten.

Charles and his bishops forced on the Scots a Prayer Book modelled on the English one, causing a riot in 1637 (below). The Scots vowed to defend their Presbyterian style of worship, leading to the Bishops' Wars.

Scotland and Ireland
The conflicts of the Civil War were fought in Scotland and Ireland as well as England and Wales. The Scots sent an army that fought on Parliament's side, and the Earl of Montrose (1612–1650) led a brief Royalist revival in Scotland in 1644–1645. The Catholic Irish, their anger fuelled by England's plantation policy, also rebelled. Both Irish and Scots were crushed by Cromwell, Parliament's most successful general.

The Trial of the King
Parliament's army leaders hoped to reach an agreement with the captured king. But when they discovered that he was secretly plotting with the Scots, who invaded England in 1648, agreement became impossible. Charles was tried as a traitor. Strictly speaking, this was illegal, but he was convicted. The public execution of Charles I in Whitehall, on 30 January 1649, shocked the Scots and all of Europe. Earlier kings had been killed, but they were murdered out of public view.

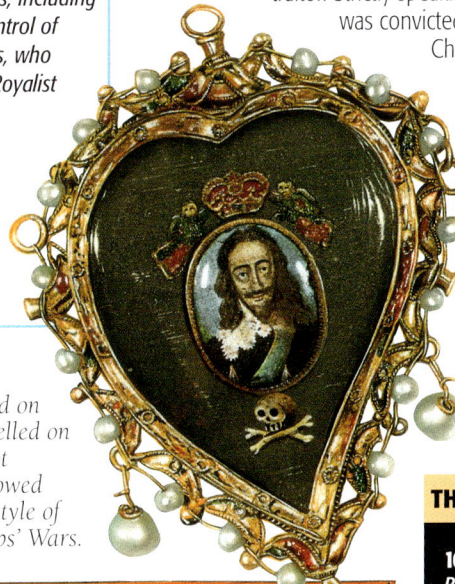

Commemorative locket containing a piece of cloth stained with the king's blood.

The Commonwealth
After Charles' execution, the main army leaders found Parliament just as difficult to deal with as Charles had done. Eventually, Oliver Cromwell expelled Parliament altogether and ruled with the title Lord Protector—not much different from a king. A country squire who had proved to be a superb general, he became one of England's greatest rulers. However, after Cromwell's death the dead king's son, Charles II, was recalled to the throne. He was to reign until his death in 1685.

THE COMMONWEALTH

1639–1640
Bishops' Wars in Scotland.

1642
Civil war in England begins.

1645
Parliament victorious at Battle of Naseby.

1649
Charles II proclaimed king of Scots in Edinburgh.

1649–1650
Oliver Cromwell crushes Irish Catholic rebellion.

1653
Cromwell becomes Lord Protector.

1657
Death of Cromwell.

1660
Restoration of the English monarchy.

In spite of his strict Puritan beliefs, Oliver Cromwell was surprisingly tolerant of most opponents.

Restoration and Revolution

Charles II was succeeded to the English throne by his younger brother, James II, in 1685. James was a Roman Catholic who angered his Protestant subjects; as a result he lost his throne in 1688 and fled into exile. The closest Protestant heir was Mary, James' daughter, who was married to the Dutch prince William of Orange. Mary and William sailed to England and ruled it jointly until Mary's death in 1694; William III died in 1702. During the reign of Queen Anne (1702–1714), England and Scotland were at last united.

The Restoration

In 1660, the English monarchy was restored, but with less power than it had in 1640. Charles II was determined to keep his crown and did not make policies without Parliament's consent. Although himself a secret Catholic who accepted money from Louis XIV of France, the great enemy of Protestant Europe, Charles agreed to a law banning Catholics from holding public office. Puritan strictness was relaxed; theaters reopened, but Charles' government imposed press censorship.

Plague and Fire

London was unhealthy, overcrowded, and dirty. In 1665, an epidemic of plague killed 56,000 people. The next year, a fire in a baker's shop spread out of control and destroyed most of the city. The disaster had some positive results: London was rebuilt in brick, rather than wood, and the new buildings by Sir Christopher Wren (1632–1723), including St Paul's Cathedral, are to this day among London's finest.

Charles II is portrayed on this earthenware pot made to celebrate the restoration of the monarchy in England.

The Great Fire of London, 1666. The diarist John Evelyn (1620–1706) watched from the south side of the River Thames. He wrote that it was "a dismal spectacle, the whole city in dreadful flames…"

Rising Prosperity

After 1660, there were fewer restrictions on business. This allowed the growth of new economic institutions such as the Bank of England. By 1700 trade—and the colonies that often grew up as a result of trade—flourished and reached new parts of the world. The British East India Company became the greatest corporation in the country. In turn, the growth of trade encouraged shipbuilding, insurance, and other types of business.

Imports of tea, coffee and cocoa from Asia led to the opening of coffee houses in English towns, where people could chat, smoke pipes, and read newspapers.

ENGLAND 1660–1705

1662
The Royal Society (of learned scientists) receives its royal charter.

1665–1667; 1672–1674
Wars against the Dutch over trade.

1678
The Popish Plot — supposed to be a Catholic plot to murder Charles II, but actually an invention by Protestants to stir trouble.

1685
Unsuccessful rebellion against James II, led by the Duke of Monmouth (1649–1685).

1695
Bank of England founded.

1701
Act of Settlement ensures that future monarchs are Protestant.

1702
The first daily newspaper is published.

The Glorious Revolution

James II was very unpopular because he was a Catholic and attempted to increase royal power. The prospect of a Catholic succession encouraged leading men to invite William of Orange to take the Crown. William's army marched into London and James fled. This changeover of monarchs, without a shot being fired, is known as the Glorious Revolution.

In 1678, Charles II gave the East India Company the authority to begin minting its own coins, called Bombay rupees.

William of Orange (William III) lands at Torbay in November 1688, with an army he never needed.

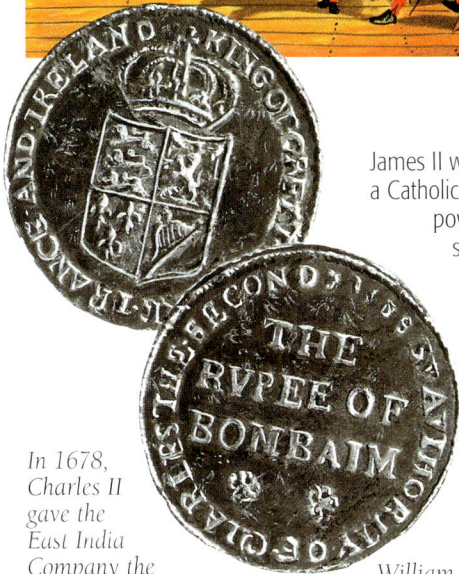

The Union of England and Scotland

At the end of the 17th century, the English and Scots were drawn closer together. Leading Scots hoped to share in England's prosperity, while the English needed Scottish agreement to the Protestant succession. Commissioners to discuss a union were appointed by Queen Anne, and the Act of Union itself was passed in 1707 against the protests of most ordinary Scots (many remained loyal to the family of the former king, James II). Scotland kept its own systems of law, education and religion.

Queen Anne receives the Act of Union, which created the new state of Great Britain.

Samuel Pepys (1633–1703), an official in the Navy Office, kept private diaries that give us a vivid picture of what life was like in Restoration London.

France in the Early 17th Century

The spectacular rise of France in the 1600s was the result of a strong central government headed by an all-powerful king. This emerged after the ravages of the Wars of Religion that tore France apart during the 1500s. The power of royal government was created not by a king, but by several ministers, especially Cardinal Richelieu (1585–1642). By 1648, France was Europe's greatest power.

Henri IV (1553–1610) was the first king of the Bourbon dynasty. To win his capital, Paris, he became a Catholic. He is said to have remarked, "Paris is worth a Mass."

The Rule of Henri IV

King Henri of Navarre inherited the French crown in 1589. Although a Huguenot, he converted to Catholicism to become accepted as king. In 1598, he ended the Religious Wars by issuing the Edict of Nantes and began the task of national recovery. The royal finances were restored by his able minister, the Duc de Sully (1560–1641), but in 1610, Henri was assassinated. His son, Louis XIII (reigned 1614–1643), was just nine years old.

Marie de Médicis Disembarking at Marseille, by Rubens. Marie (1573–1642), daughter of the Grand Duke of Tuscany, married Henri IV in 1600.

The Pont Neuf was the first Parisian bridge built without buildings across the top. Henri IV is commemorated by a mounted statue beside the bridge.

A plot to kill Huguenot leaders on the eve of St Bartholomew's Day (23 August) 1572 turned into a massacre of Protestants. About 3,000 died in Paris alone.

The Wars of Religion

The civil wars between French Catholics and Protestant Huguenots lasted nearly 40 years. Apart from the bloodshed, the wars did great harm to France. Farming suffered, and finance and government both became hopelessly corrupt: government jobs were sold to the highest bidders, who treated them simply as opportunities to make money.

Portrait of Louis XIII.

Rise of French Power

While Louis XIII was still a boy, his mother, Marie de Médicis, ruled as regent from 1610 until 1614. But she wasted Sully's good work and allowed profiteers to dominate government. Her influence ended when Louis took full power in 1617. By that time, an ambitious and gifted priest in royal service, Cardinal Richelieu, was becoming influential. In 1624, Richelieu was made first minister—in effect the ruler of France. He was wise, far-sighted and ruthless, and his aims were to crush the Huguenots and the troublesome nobles, to make the monarchy supreme and France great once again. He largely succeeded in his aims.

Armand Jean de Plessis, better known as the Cardinal and Duc de Richelieu, influenced every aspect of French life, including the economy and the arts.

French Society

In the early 17th century, France suffered many revolts and civil conflicts, due partly to the continuing religious divisions, but also to the desperation of poor people without enough to live on. Even a minister as clever as Richelieu could not prevent plague and famine, although for him foreign policy was more important. He wanted greater prosperity so that he could raise taxes to support his foreign enterprises. His greatest ability was as a diplomat and a statesman, rather than administrator.

Return from Haymaking, by Louis Le Nain (c. 1593–1648). Peasants formed by far the biggest section of the population, and they were the poorest, too. Pictures like this one give us some idea of what ordinary people's lives were like.

The Sun King

Louis XIV was the richest and most powerful ruler in Europe, and reigned for longer than any other—from 1643 until 1715. This was a glorious period in French history, not least in sciences, literature and the arts. Louis's court was so ceremonious and dazzling that it earned him the name "the Sun King." The expense of his many wars, however, was very damaging for France.

The End of the Huguenots

Louis was a zealous Catholic who steadily excluded the Huguenots from public life. Heavy fines and the practice of making Huguenot households give lodging to soldiers forced many of them to convert. The Edict of Nantes, which guaranteed Huguenot rights, was finally revoked in 1685, so thousands fled to England and other Protestant countries.

A Huguenot is forced to convert to Catholicism at gunpoint. Many of the Huguenots who fled France were skilled craftsmen and businessmen.

The Early Years

Louis became king at the age of five. His mother acted as regent, supported by Cardinal Mazarin (1602–1661). Mazarin was the follower and successor of Richelieu and ruled until his death, when Louis took over. Mazarin's diplomatic skills made France the strongest country in Europe. He also encouraged Louis's belief in himself as an absolute ruler, who answered only to God.

His fortune, Italian birth, and taxation policies made Mazarin unpopular. He was briefly driven from power during the Frondes.

The Frondes

Civil wars, known as the Frondes, broke out again in 1648. They were caused by Mazarin's unpopularity with the Parlement and the nobles, who had lost power to the monarchy. During the chaos, a mob broke into the palace in Paris. This made Louis determined to introduce stronger rule and to build a new, grander palace.

Louis XIV's Wars

The strength of France made other countries uneasy, and French attempts at expansion, partly to guard its northern borders, caused a series of wars between European alliances. For a time, the French army seemed invincible, but the War of the Spanish Succession (1702–1714) brought final defeat.

The expansion of France:

- 1648
- 1659
- 1661
- 1668
- 1678–1679
- Temporary gains 1684–1697
- 1697
- Holy Roman Empire border

FRANCE IN 1648–1715

ENGLAND · ENGLISH CHANNEL · FLANDERS · HOLY ROMAN EMPIRE · TOURNAI · LUXEMBOURG · DUCHY OF LORRAINE (occupied 1670–1697) · PARIS · ORLÉANS · STRASBOURG · FRANCHE COMTÉ · NANTES · POITIERS · ATLANTIC OCEAN · BORDEAUX · LYON · TOULOUSE · AVIGNON · NICE · SPAIN · MEDITERRANEAN SEA

The Palace of Versailles

The new royal palace at Versailles, just outside Paris, was one of the wonders of the world. Its sheer size stunned foreign ambassadors. The gardens contained more than 1,000 fountains. The palace was large enough to house the entire French ruling class, which kept them away from Paris and their own estates, and effectively turned them into royal attendants. Life was lived according to strict and lengthy ceremonies, and must have been quite dull.

The Palace of Versailles as it appeared in 1675. Louis and his court moved there in 1682.

Louis's idle courtiers take a stroll in the splendid new formal gardens of the Tuileries, Paris.

Louis XIV's royal authority was complete: the nobles were powerless and the representative assemblies were never summoned.

France Under Louis XIV

Louis XIV reigned during a rich period in French culture. The king's love of order was echoed in the classical spirit of the times, especially in the visual arts, literature, and music. His leading minister, Jean Baptiste Colbert (1619–1683), increased the wealth of France through trade and industry, established the Royal Academy of Painting and Sculpture, and introduced a new code of law. But Colbert failed to improve the country's unfair tax system.

SPAIN UNDER PHILIP III

1604
Peace with England is agreed.

1609
Truce with the Dutch.

1615
Philip III's daughter, Anne of Austria, marries Louis XIII (see page 20).

1618
Duke of Lerma dismissed from the royal court.

1619
Madrid's Plaza Mayor (Great Square) is built.

1620
Spain enters the Thirty Years' War.

1621
War with the Dutch is renewed.

Spain in Europe

Under Philip III, Spain still behaved as though it were the strongest and richest power in Europe. It had agents and supporters in every capital city—even Protestant capitals. The haughty Castilian nobles who represented Spain abroad considered Spain supreme, and its vast empire seemed set to grow still larger with the promise of Tirol (now western Austria) and Alsace at the Treaty of Graz in 1617. However, later events prevented the handover from happening.

Foreign Affairs

Spain had been at war with the Protestant Dutch, who were revolting against Spanish rule, since 1568. Economic difficulties prompted Spain to call a temporary truce in 1609, which made eventual Dutch independence a certainty.
The Duke of Lerma also ended 16 years of conflict with England, and narrowly avoided war with France. But Spain urgently needed reforms at home, and Lerma was not the man to achieve reform. Spain's disastrous entry into the Thirty Years' War occurred under Lerma's successor.

The Spanish Armada, the fleet sent by Philip II in 1588 to invade England and bring an end to the English war, suffered a huge defeat. This heavy blow forced the Spanish, the mightiest European naval power of the time, to build an improved navy.

This statue of Philip III was designed by the Italian sculptor Giambologna (1529–1608). It stands in Plaza Mayor in Madrid.

The Duke of Lerma was an undistinguished nobleman whose enormous personal wealth made him very unpopular with the overtaxed Spaniards.

Spain Under Philip III

Philip III became king of Spain in 1598 at the age of 20, and reigned until 1621. He inherited the largest empire the world had yet seen, and a position as political leader of Catholic Europe. Like his father, Philip II (reigned 1556–1598), he was a devoted Catholic. But, unlike him, did not enjoy the dull work of government. Instead Philip III left it to a royal favourite, the Duke of Lerma (1553–1625). During Philip's reign Spain's "Golden Age," which had begun during the Renaissance, continued.

Detail from an early painting by the young Velásquez, when he painted realistic pictures of peasants rather than nobles and courtiers.

The Spanish Golden Age

Spain under Philip III was still in its "Golden Age," with brilliant achievements in literature and art. Cervantes published *Don Quixote* in 1605, Lope de Vega (1562–1635) wrote hundreds of mostly good plays, and Diego Velásquez (1599–1660), working in Seville, became court painter in 1623. Besides religious pursuits, Philip III's successor, Philip IV (reigned 1621–1665), enjoyed elaborate court festivities. But despite all the glamor, the government was deep in debt.

Society and Economy

So much silver had flowed into Spain from the Americas that people felt less inclined to work hard in industry or on farms. Famine in Castile was followed by plague, Spain was still at war in the Netherlands, and taxes were increased. Meanwhile, the Duke of Lerma was forced to borrow money against Spain's future income. Eventually, he debased the coinage, substituting copper for silver.

This Spanish silver coin was minted during the reign of Philip III. Imported American silver had made Spain rich.

The Expulsion of the Moriscos

Moriscos were Spanish Muslims who had officially "converted" to Christianity, but who privately remained loyal Muslims. Unpopular with Spanish Catholics and suspected of plotting against the government, about 275,000 of them were expelled to North Africa in 1609–1614. They were mostly small farmers and tradesmen. Their loss caused a crisis in Aragon and Valencia, where they had formed a quarter of the population.

The expulsion of the Moriscos was popular with ordinary people, but damaging to Spain. Even less food was grown after they had left the country.

The Spanish Decline

During the 17th century, the weakness in Spain's economy and society, present since the reign of Philip II, increased until it overwhelmed the country. Spain's "Golden Age" ended, France took over as the leading European power, rebellions broke out, and many Spanish territories were lost. By 1705, foreign armies were marching on Spanish soil.

EUROPEAN TERRITORIAL CHANGES

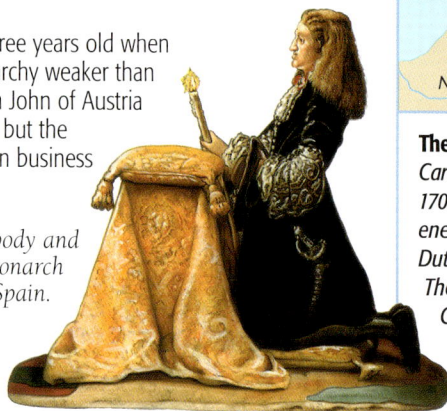

🟥	To Spain
🟧	To Austria
🟪	To France
🟩	To Savoy
🟥	To Prussia
🟩	To Britain
•	Major battle

The Reign of Carlos II

Carlos II (reigned 1665–1700) was just three years old when he came to the throne, making the monarchy weaker than ever. Until 1679, his uncle, the pro-French John of Austria (1629–1679), controlled the government, but the economy did not improve. Most people in business were foreigners, mainly French.

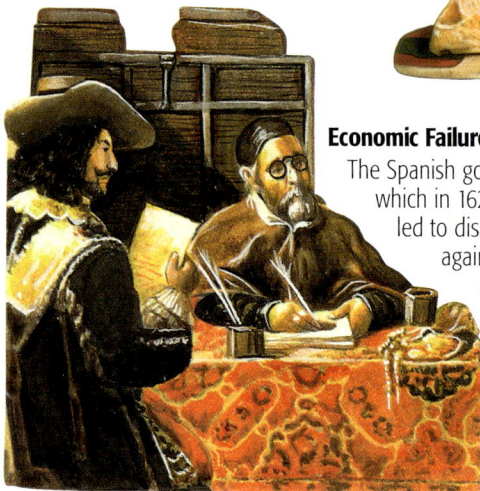

Carlos II at prayer. Carlos, weak in body and mind, was the last Habsburg monarch to rule in Spain.

The Spanish Succession

Carlos II left the Spanish crown to Philip of Anjou (Philip V, reigned 1700–1746), the grandson of Louis XIV of France. But all the leading enemies of Louis XIV, including England, the Austrian empire and the Dutch, objected to a member of the French dynasty ruling Spain. They supported the claim of an Austrian candidate, the Archduke Charles (1685–1740), and so the War of the Spanish Succession (1701–1714) broke out. English and Austrian armies won many battles against the French. In the end Philip V kept the throne, but Spain and France emerged weaker and Britain stronger.

Economic Failure

The Spanish government continued its risky policy of manipulating the coinage, which in 1628 caused a collapse of prices. In 1641–1642, bad management again led to disastrous deflation. Industry declined. The Catalans rebelled, partly against government efforts to get them to pay more taxes for defence. Naples (a Spanish possession) rebelled in 1647 for similar reasons. Falling trade with American colonies also reduced Spain's income.

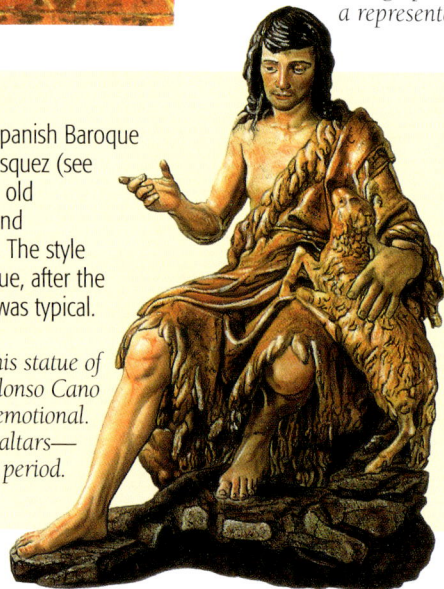

A tax collector records the amounts paid or owed under the watchful eye of a high-ranking Spanish nobleman, a representative of the king.

Spanish Baroque

In painting, the style known as Spanish Baroque reached its peak with Diego Velásquez (see also page 25). In architecture, the old Spanish liking for bold, ornate, and imaginative decoration returned. The style sometimes called Churrigueresque, after the work of the Churriguera family, was typical.

Spanish sculpture, such as in this statue of John the Baptist by Alonso Cano (1601–1667), was strongly emotional. Cano also designed spectacular altars— a Spanish speciality in this period.

The altar of the church of San Esteban in Salamanca, by José Benito de Churriguera (1665–1725), is an example of the highly decorative Spanish Baroque style of architecture.

French Victory

In 1643, Spain's fortunes in the Thirty Years' War suffered a crushing blow at the hands of the French in the battle of Rocroi. This ended the belief that Spain's infantry was invincible. The French war effort was disrupted by civil strife at home, allowing the Spanish to carry on until the Treaty of the Pyrenees (1659) ended the war.

The Count-Duke Olivares, painted by Velásquez in 1634.

The Velázquez painting below, titled Las Meniñas *(meaning "maids of honor"), shows the painter at work alongside the royal children of Philip IV. The image of the king and queen is reflected in the mirror.*

The Reign of Philip IV

Philip IV was a generous patron of art and literature, but he left government to his minister, the Count-Duke Olivares (1587–1645). Determined to restore Spain's greatness, Olivares tried to centralize government in Madrid. This provoked a revolt in Catalonia, while Portugal at last regained independence after 60 years of Spanish rule (see pages 28–29). The cost of the Thirty Years' War was ruinous, and the bankrupt government was run by an a cabal of dishonest officials.

A coin bearing the head of Philip IV.

THE END OF AN ERA

1640
Portugal regains its independence.

1647
Revolt in Naples.

1648
Spain acknowledges Dutch independence at the Treaty of Westphalia.

1652
Spain regains Catalonia after its long struggle for independence from the rest of Spain.

c. 1656
Velázquez paints Las Meniñas.

1667
France invades Spanish Netherlands (modern Belgium).

1680
Pueblo revolt against the Spanish in New Mexico (now part of the USA).

1683
New French invasion of Spanish Netherlands.

Portugal

The first European nation to explore the oceans in search of trade, Portugal set up outposts in Africa, India and the Far East. Two great empire builders, Francisco de Almeida (1450–1510) and Afonso de Albuquerque (1453–1515), created a commercial empire stretching from Brazil to China with its headquarters at Goa, India. Most of it was lost to the Dutch in the 17th century.

King Sebastião (reigned 1557–1578) invaded North Africa with a badly organized army, which the Muslims easily defeated.

A gold São Vincente coin of João III (reigned 1502–1557). It shows St Vincent, who was the patron saint of Portugal and of navigation, holding a Portuguese exploration ship.

PORTUGAL

1580
Philip II of Spain becomes king of Portugal.

1615
The Dutch capture the Spice Islands (Moluccas) from the Portuguese.

1640–1656
Reign of João IV of Portugal.

1654
The Portuguese regain Brazil from The Dutch.

1656–1683
Reign of Afonso VI.

1661
Treaty of alliance with England

1683–1706
Reign of Pedro II.

1693
Gold is discovered in Brazil.

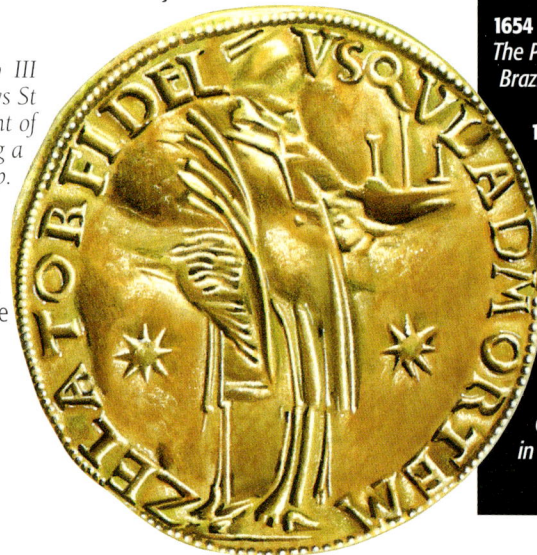

Independence Lost

In 1578, King Sebastião disappeared while on a religious crusade in North Africa. He had no heir, so his mighty neighbor, Philip II of Spain, seized the Portuguese throne (as Philip I). Spanish rule was unpopular. Many Portuguese, unhappy at losing their independence, hoped Sebastião was still alive and would return to reclaim his throne.

Under Spanish Rule

The Spanish link was supposed to bring economic gains, but it had serious disadvantages. The Dutch, at war with Spain and now unable to trade with Portugal, invaded Portugal's overseas colonies. The Portuguese had to pay taxes for Spain's expensive wars. Philip II's promise to allow them to run their own country was broken by his successors.

Lisbon, the Portuguese capital, had trade links that spanned the world, but most were lost under Spanish rule.

The Portuguese Revolt

A genuine claimant to the Portuguese throne (several imposters claiming to be "Sebastião" had already appeared) was found in the Duke of Braganza (1604–1656). Encouraged by French secret agents, and furious at a plan of the Spanish minister Olivares to make Portuguese soldiers fight Spanish rebels, Portuguese leaders led a nationalist rebellion in Braganza's favour in 1640. The Spaniards were driven out and the duke was crowned as King João IV, although a long and bitter war followed.

The armor of Pedro II, made by an English armorer in London in c. 1683. Its decoration includes the cross of the commander of the Order of Christ, a title inherited by the kings of Portugal.

Independent Portugal

Spain finally recognised Portugal's independence in the Treaty of Lisbon of 1668. Spain was weakening and João IV was widely recognised as the rightful king abroad and in the colonies. The marriage of his daughter, Catherine of Braganza, to Charles II of England renewed an old English alliance. Unfortunately, João's successor, Afonso VI (reigned 1656–1683), was feeble-minded. Afonso's French wife fell for his more attractive brother Pedro, and arranged to have her marriage to Afonso annulled. She then married Pedro, who acted as regent for his brother until he finally succeeded him as King Pedro II in 1683.

The baroque portal of the church of Santa Maria de Belém in Lisbon.

Portrait of Catherine of Braganza. Her wedding dowry included the Indian port of Bombay, which became the headquarters of the British East India Company.

Seal of Catherine of Braganza (1638–1705), the Portuguese wife of Charles II of England. She married Charles in 1662 and outlived him by 20 years.

The Portuguese Empire

Portugal had become a world power in the 16th century despite having a population of less than two million, and it was never so strong again. Although the Dutch were to drive the Portuguese from their Asian colonies, Portugal retained large (mainly unexplored) territories in southern Africa and South America. Brazil produced gold and precious stones, helping to make Portugal more prosperous. Later, in 1728, diamonds were found in Brazil, too.

The Revolt of the Netherlands

The Netherlands were part of the Habsburg empire inherited by Philip II of Spain in 1555. The Netherlanders disliked Catholic Spanish rule for its persecution of Protestants, a majority in this part of Europe. A Spanish reign of terror finally provoked a revolt in 1568, and, after a long war, the Netherlands declared independence as the United Provinces. However, the more Catholic south (modern Belgium) remained under Spanish rule as the Spanish Netherlands.

The War of Independence

The Dutch won victories against Spanish forces on land thanks to a brilliant general, Maurice of Nassau (1567–1625), and at sea thanks to their "Sea Beggars," a kind of part-time navy. They had some support from Protestant England and their efforts were aided by a huge economic boom, centered in Amsterdam. The war was fought, on and off, for nearly 80 years. Spain did not officially recognize Dutch independence until 1648.

THE NETHERLANDS

1576
Rebellious Spanish soldiers go on rampage in Antwerp and kill 7,000.

1584
Assassination of Dutch leader, William the Silent, Prince of Orange.

1602
The Dutch East India Company is founded.

1609
Twelve-year Truce is agreed with Spain.

1652
Cape Town is founded.

1672
France invades the Netherlands.

1666
A Dutch admiral boldly seizes the English navy's flagship at its port.

1689
William III, Prince of Orange, becomes king of England.

The Dutch Empire

During the 1600s, the Dutch East India Company took over Portuguese colonies and trading posts in Africa, Asia and South America. The Dutch also conquered some Spanish colonies, such as Curaçao in the Caribbean, and set up their own—including New Netherland on the East Coast of America (later renamed New York) and Cape Town, at the southern tip of Africa. By 1672, Louis XIV of France had replaced Spain as the major threat to the growth of the Netherlands.

The final Dutch victory over the Spanish caused much rejoicing in the Netherlands. This salt-cellar was made to celebrate the occasion.

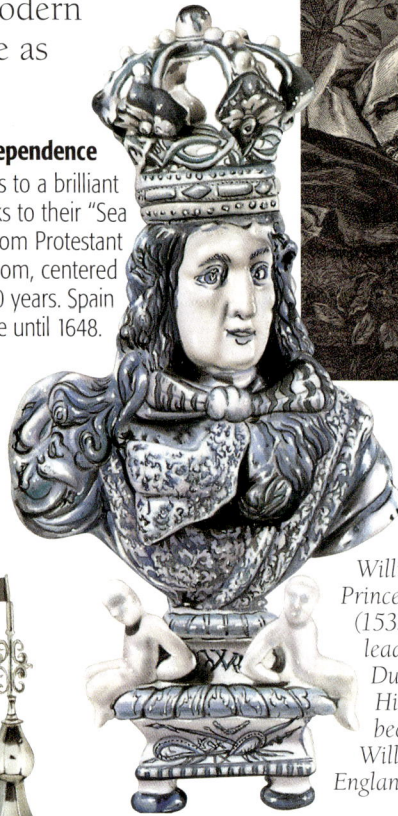

The wealthy middle class liked to have their portraits painted by fine Dutch painters. This example is by Frans Hals (1580–1666).

William the Silent, the Prince of Orange (1533–1584), was a leading figure of the Dutch revolt. His great-grandson became King William III of England in 1689.

The Middle Class

In the Netherlands, the nobles were not so grand and arrogant nor so numerous as they were in France, for example. Instead, the republic drew its strength from its large and educated middle class—the chief money earners.

This detail from a painting by the Spanish artist Velásquez shows the surrender of Breda, a Dutch port, to the Spanish in 1625.

The United Provinces

The Dutch Republic was formed from seven united provinces. Holland, which contained nearly all of the biggest towns, was the largest and most powerful of these. Each province was represented in the States General, but governed itself. The States General were flanked by the Stadtholder, who was elected. Although small, the republic was the leading sea power in Europe, with the most successful economy.

AN INDEPENDENT DUTCH REPUBLIC

- Dutch republic
- Spanish control
- Independent principalities

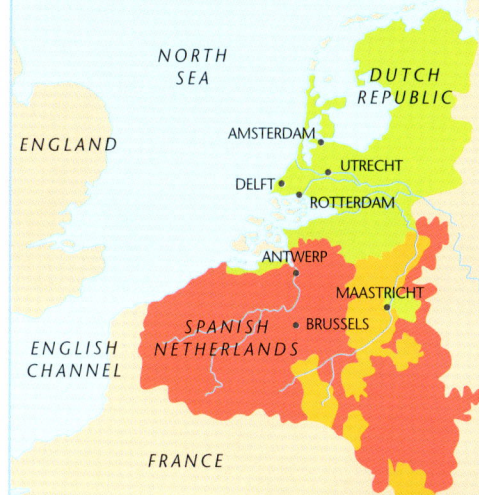

NORTH SEA
DUTCH REPUBLIC
ENGLAND
AMSTERDAM
UTRECHT
DELFT
ROTTERDAM
ANTWERP
MAASTRICHT
SPANISH NETHERLANDS
BRUSSELS
ENGLISH CHANNEL
FRANCE

Shipbuilding was the greatest Dutch manufacturing industry. The largest merchant ships were more than 20,000 tons.

International Trade

The great economic success of the Dutch was based on shipping. Three-quarters of world trade was carried in Dutch ships, while Amsterdam became a major international port and Europe's main financial center. Its population, buildings, shipyard, and canals all grew enormously. The tolerant city attracted refugees from religious persecution, and it also benefited from the decline of the maritime city-states, Venice and Genoa. But its rivalry with England overseas caused three short naval wars between 1652 and 1674.

The busy harborside at Amsterdam, which enjoyed a secure position and had access to world trade routes.

The Town Hall (now the Royal Palace) in Amsterdam, designed by Jacob van Campen (1595–1657) and built in about 1655, was supported on 13,659 huge wooden piles.

The Dutch Golden Age

While the Dutch were fighting for independence from Spain and creating their own republic, they also entered a golden age in Dutch history. The fast-growing prosperity of towns and trade encouraged remarkable developments in culture. Painting is the best-known example, but great advances also took place in architecture, exploration, law, and science.

Detail of Rembrandt's A Young Painter in His Studio *(1629). The "young painter" is Rembrandt himself.*

Amsterdam

Seventeenth-century Amsterdam was booming. Its population rose by 300 percent in 50 years, and it attracted talented people from many places. Built on swampy ground, its large buildings were supported on wooden posts known as piles, each the size of a ship's mainmast. The architecture was a simpler, Protestant version of Baroque, but with decorated gables along the rooftops. The Hague, Delft, Haarlem, Leiden, and Utrecht also expanded rapidly at this time.

Dutch Painting

Many Dutch artists traveled to Italy and were inspired by the great Italian artists of the Renaissance. Today, however, we associate Dutch painting more with the realists who painted ordinary people, domestic scenes, and everyday life. Perhaps the most famous of these is Jan Vermeer (1632–1675) of Delft. However, greatest of all Dutch painters was Rembrandt Harmenszoon van Rijn, who painted widely differing subjects, including many portraits and self-portraits.

A Cultured People

Although the first Dutch university, at Leiden, was not founded until 1575, middle- and upper-class people were well educated and had wide interests. The handsome and athletic Constantijn Huygens (1596–1687) was a typical Dutch gentleman of the time: secretary to the Stadtholder, patron of Rembrandt, he spoke the main European languages, wrote poetry and philosophy, and played the lute.

The Dutch were keen collectors, which partly explains the large number of painters. Apart from paintings, successful people also collected "curiosities" like this gilded snail— objects of artistic, scientific, or cultural interest.

Detail of the portrait titled The Girl with the Pearl Earring *(c. 1665) by Vermeer. Only about 35 of his works survive today. They are famous for their realism and serenity.*

Religion

The only recognised church in the United Provinces was strictly Calvinist. Religious quarrels marked the early history of the republic. But Amsterdam, where business was the most important occupation, practised religious toleration. The city also benefited economically from the refugees–French Huguenots, Spanish Jews and even some English groups–who fled there to escape persecution.

In the 1630s "tulipmania" broke out in Amsterdam and the value of these rare new flowers skyrocketed. Many Dutch businessmen looking for a get-rich-quick scheme invested fortunes in the flowers' cultivation. By 1637, however, the tulip craze was over, and many of these investors went bankrupt.

Medal commemorating the Synod of Dort (Dordrecht) of 1618–1619. This national assembly had gathered to judge the religious dispute. It favored the Calvinist Church against more liberal believers, known as the "Remonstrants."

Business and Finance

The economic boom encouraged the development of banks to finance trading ventures. The Bank of Amsterdam was founded in 1609. It acted as a place where claims and accounts between different parties were settled, and as a currency exchange. It lent money to big institutions such as the city of Amsterdam or the hugely successful East India Company. Similar banks were soon founded in other cities.

Traders discussing business in Amsterdam's stock exchange, built in 1613.

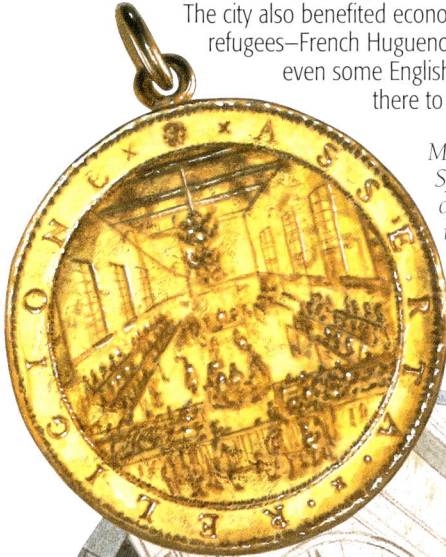

The Italian States

For much of the early 1500s, Spain and France struggled for control over Italy, until, in 1559, the treaty of Cateau-Cambrésis left Spain the dominant power in the peninsula. Spain ruled directly over Milan, Naples, Sicily, and Sardinia, and influenced many other Italian regions. In spite of differences, Spain was generally an ally of the pope. During the 17th century, the enterprise and energy of Renaissance Italy faded.

Statue of David (1623) by Bernini, who worked mainly in Rome.

Italian Art
The Baroque style originated in Italy, and its purest form, the so-called "High Baroque," is rarely found anywhere else. The style was at its peak in about 1630–1680, when it united architecture, painting, and sculpture. Its most famous exponent was Gianlorenzo Bernini (1598–1680). The High Baroque blended light, color, and movement, and gave an appearance of striking realism, making a strong appeal to the viewer's emotions.

Spanish Rule
In Italy as in Spain, taxation was heavy, the economy was in decline, and much-needed reforms were not being made. Increases in food prices provoked a serious revolt in Naples against the government in 1647. A Neapolitan republic, backed by the French, was declared by the rebels, but Spanish forces crushed the revolt in 1648. Milan experienced frequent riots, and Florence, once the heart of European culture, went into decline.

A fisherman known as Masaniello (1622–1647) headed the Naples revolt in May 1647, but was murdered months later.

ITALY

1559
Treaty of Cateau-Cambrésis.

1605
Venice rejects papal authority in its secular government.

1647
Revolt in Naples.

1670
Cosimo III (1642–1723) becomes Grand Duke of Tuscany. Period of decline in Tuscany begins.

1684
Louis XIV orders the bombardment of Genoa.

1699
Treaty of Karlowitz confirms Venetian control of the Peloponnese, a large peninsula in southern Greece.

1700
Death of the last Habsburg king of Spain.

ITALY IN THE MID-17TH CENTURY

DUCHY OF SAVOY
MILAN
REPUBLIC OF VENICE
OTTOMAN EMPIRE
VENICE
PARMA
GENOA
FLORENCE
PAPAL STATES
ADRIATIC SEA
CORSICA
ROME
NAPLES
REPUBLIC OF NAPLES
SARDINIA
MEDITERRANEAN SEA
PALERMO
SICILY
NORTH AFRICA

	Venice		Venetian control		Direct Spanish rule		Papal states
	French control		Spanish control		Independent states		

Italian States
In the mid-1600s, Savoy was still under French influence. The small states of central Italy, such as Ferrara, Mantua, and Parma, were independent but had little influence. The Papal States were hemmed in by Spanish territory, and the papacy, steering a diplomatic course between France and Spain, lacked the power it had in Medieval times. When the Treaty of Westphalia awarded many Church estates to Protestants in 1648, the Pope protested in vain. Papal efforts to renew the Crusades were also a failure.

Portrait of Cosimo II de' Medici (1590–1621), the Grand Duke of Tuscany, made from gem stones. Cosimo closed the Medici Bank, the source of the family's power. After his reign the family's fortunes gradually declined.

Seventeenth-century musical innovations, such as the introduction of the violin and the creation of opera, spread across Europe from the Italian courts. The great violin maker Antonio Stradivari (1644–1737) made this example in 1693.

Decline of Power at Sea

Genoa was a great trading city throughout the Middle Ages, but it had been losing power, territory, and wealth ever since. Although it was still independent in name, it was under Spanish influence and it declined after the Spanish crown went bankrupt. Venice, too, had lost its former glory. Its trade was damaged by war with the Ottoman Turks, who captured Crete in 1669, and by competition from the new sea routes that led south through the Atlantic Ocean and on to the Far East.

Venice's stone Rialto Bridge was built over the Grand Canal in 1588–1591. It replaced the old wooden bridge. The Rialto area was the city's busiest center for trade and banking.

Most 17th-century scientists, such as this scholar in Vermeer's painting, were amateurs who had time and curiosity to spare.

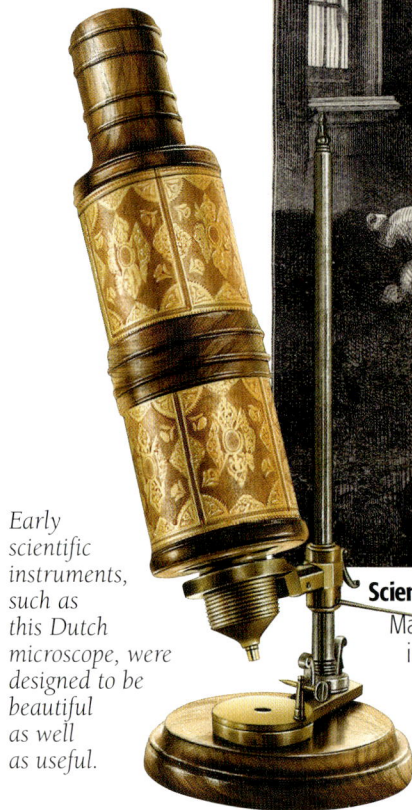

Early scientific instruments, such as this Dutch microscope, were designed to be beautiful as well as useful.

Scientific Instruments
Many of the recently invented, or improved, instruments were made in the Netherlands, where a lot of the new discoveries also took place. They included the telescope, microscope, timekeepers such as pendulum clocks, thermometers, and various navigational and measuring instruments.

Earth and the Universe
Nicolaus Copernicus (1473–1543) explained how the Earth moves around the Sun in 1543, but the Church still rejected his explanation. Galileo was later forced to deny it by the Inquisition, yet most well-educated people accepted it, especially after Tycho Brahe (1546–1601) and Johannes Kepler (1571–1630) made major new discoveries.

The Universe Explained
Italian physicist Galileo Galilei (1564–1642) was a great observer. He discovered the principle of the pendulum by watching a swinging lamp. Hearing about the Dutch invention of a telescope, he made a better one. He observed the moons circling Jupiter and the mountains on our Moon. He discovered that stars form the Milky Way and look small because they are far away. The movement of heavenly bodies was finally explained by English physicist Sir Isaac Newton (1642–1727) and his theory of gravity. The orbit of the Moon, he explained, obeys the same law as an apple falling from a tree.

Modern Science

Europe in the 17th century underwent a revolution in scientific discovery. Islamic countries, India and China were all more advanced that Europe in 1600, but Europeans soon began to catch up. In 1620, the English scholar Francis Bacon (1561–1626) defined the scientific method as: observation, which gives rise to theory, which is tested by experiment. This new approach led to many discoveries, marking the beginning of modern science.

The sheer number of Galileo's observations greatly increased human knowledge of the universe.

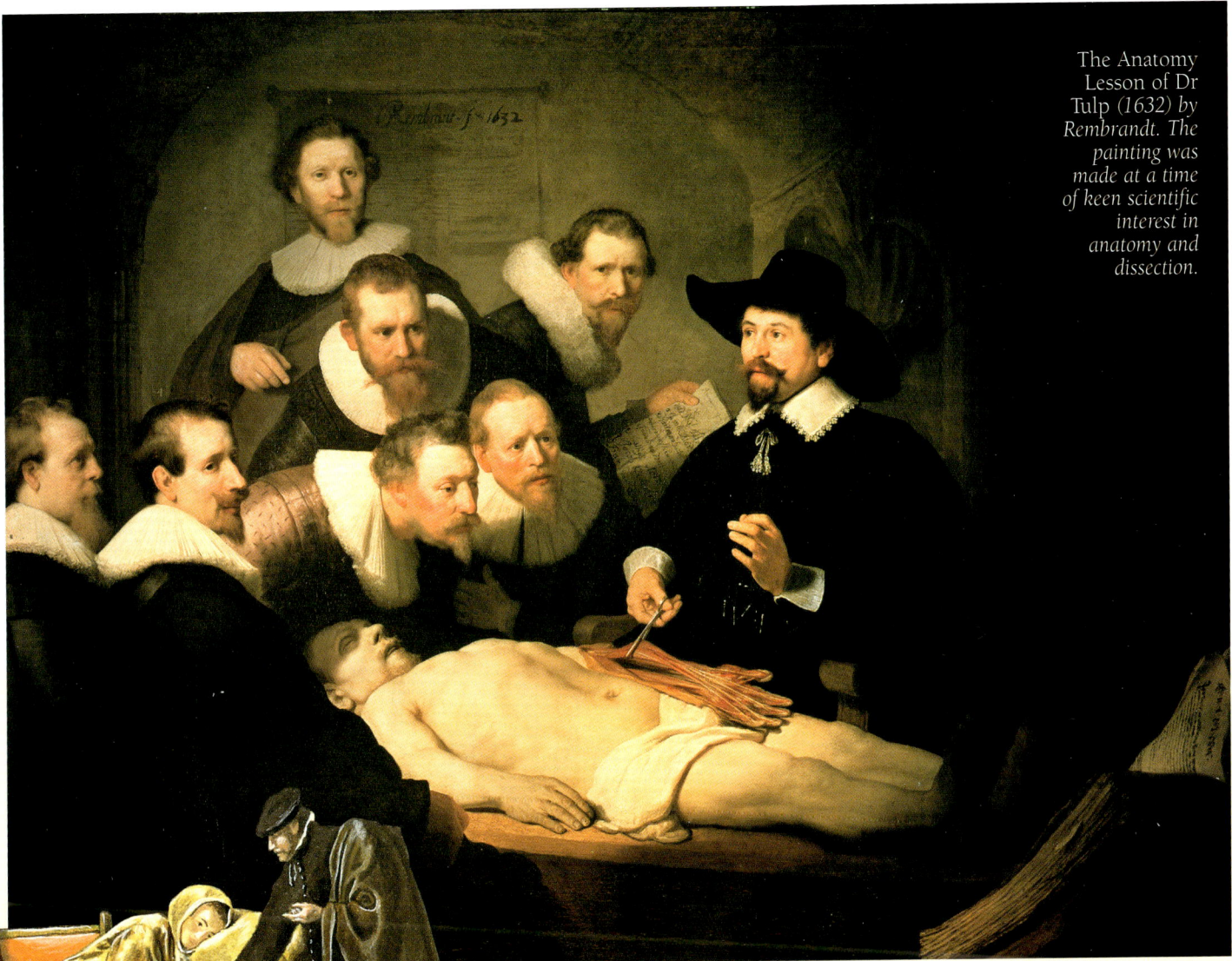

The Anatomy Lesson of Dr Tulp (1632) by Rembrandt. The painting was made at a time of keen scientific interest in anatomy and dissection.

A physician checks his patient's heart beat in this painting by Jan Steen (c. 1625–1679) of the Dutch school.

Human Anatomy

A textbook of 1543 by Flemish anatomist Andreas Vesalius (1514–1564) remained the main authority on anatomy during the 17th century. The Church disapproved of dissecting human bodies, but people queued to get into lectures by famous anatomists. The lecture room was called a "theater" and was a place of both learning and entertainment.

Medicine

Medicine advanced with discoveries of how the body worked. In 1628, William Harvey (1578–1657) discovered how the blood circulates. Antoni van Leeuwenhoek (1632–1723) designed an improved microscope that allowed him to see bacteria and red blood cells. Others realised the importance of chemistry. However, superstitious ideas were still common; modern biology did not develop until the 19th century.

Scientific Societies

An important feature of 17th-century science was the foundation of learned societies, where ideas and experiments were discussed and scientists met one another. These societies also produced journals, which spread the latest knowledge more widely. The first national scientific society was the Royal Society in London (1660), followed by others in Paris (1666) and Berlin (1700).

Detail of a painting showing Louis XIV with members of the Paris Academy of Sciences. It attracted scientists from all over Europe, including the Dutch mathematician, astronomer, and physicist Christiaan Huygens (1629–1695).

Frederick III (reigned 1648–1670) benefited from a new constitution giving Danish kings more power.

Danish Absolute Monarchy

The successful defence of Copenhagen against a Swedish army in 1658 made Frederick III very popular. He was supposed to be an elected king of Denmark and Norway, but his prestige was such that, under a new constitution (1665), he became a hereditary, absolute monarch, with powers even greater than those of Louis XIV of France. The nobles lost political power, while the towns and the merchants prospered. However, the peasants, as usual, remained poor and over-taxed.

This fabulous gold crown was worn by Danish kings from Christian V (reigned 1670–1699) to Christian VIII (reigned 1839–1848).

Drottningholm Palace was built in Sweden by Queen Hedvig Eleonora (1636–1715). It is famous today for its theater, added in 1766, which is one of the oldest of its kind in Europe.

Danish-Swedish Wars

The kings of Denmark and Norway hoped to restore the old Scandinavian union, while the Swedes were interested only in a union controlled by themselves. These conflicting ambitions led to frequent wars in which Denmark was the overall loser. Christian IV of Denmark (reigned 1588–1648) entered the Thirty Years' War in 1625 on the Protestant side, but was defeated. He was a good governor and popular, but during a war with Sweden in 1643–1645 he lost Jutland and other territory—as well as an eye.

Axel Oxenstierna, the chancellor of Sweden from 1612 to 1654, worked for strong central government. He was the virtual ruler of Sweden after the death of Gustavus Adolphus (reigned 1611–1632).

Sweden, Denmark and Norway

During the 17th century, Scandinavia played its greatest role in European affairs since the Viking age. After the break-up, in 1523, of the Union of Kalmar, which had united Scandinavia under the Danish crown, Sweden gradually emerged as the dominant power in northern Europe. It won control of the Baltic from Denmark, and maintained its supremacy until 1709. Norway remained under the control of the Danish kings, but it had its own laws and institutions.

SCANDINAVIA

1621
Gustavus Adolphus of Sweden creates Europe's first modern army.

1630
Gustavus Adolphus invades Germany.

1645
The first Swedish newspaper is founded under the reign of Queen Christina.

1654
Sweden occupies Trondheim in Norway.

1658
Treaty of Roskilde between Sweden and Denmark.

1660
Constitutional revolution in Denmark. At the Peace of Copenhagen, the modern boundaries of Denmark, Sweden, and Norway are established.

1654
Abdication of Queen Christina of Sweden. Her cousin, Charles X Gustav (1622–1660), is crowned king of Sweden.

1659
Siege of Copenhagen.

1683
New system of law introduced by Christian V in Denmark.

THE EXPANSION OF SWEDEN

🟨 Denmark and Norway	Seas and lakes frozen in winter
🟪 Occupied by Sweden in 1645	Sweden in 1560
	Occupied by Sweden in 1560–1660
	Parts of Finland colonised by Sweden
🟧 Swedish occupation of Russia in 1613	➡ Principal trade route

Sweden's Rise

Sweden developed at Denmark's expense, fighting a series of wars against its former overlord in which, by 1628, it had emerged the victor, winning territory on the continental mainland. Under an extraordinary monarch, Gustavus Adolphus, and backed by an able minister, Count Oxenstierna, Sweden replaced Denmark as the Protestant champion of the Thirty Years' War (see pages 10–11), and astonished all of Europe with its victories. Gains at the treaties of Westphalia (1648) and Roskilde (1658) further enlarged the Swedish empire.

Queen Christina of Sweden

Count Oxenstierna controlled the government as guardian of the infant queen, Christina (1626–1689), and remained in power after she came of age in 1632. She was herself a remarkable, highly intelligent character, but abdicated when she became a Roman Catholic–an unacceptable thing to do in Protestant Sweden. Ex-queen Christina moved to Rome and led a lively intellectual and artistic life, while trying unsuccessfully to win the thrones of Poland and Naples.

Among the scholars of Christina's intellectual circle was the leading French philosopher René Descartes.

Poland

Many European countries adopted a system of absolute monarchy in the 17th century, but in Poland the monarchy was elected, and therefore weak. The rich and selfish nobility took bribes to vote for the favored candidates of foreign powers, and, under Poland's peculiar constitution, they could paralyse the government. Weak leadership resulted in the loss of territory to Sweden and Russia. Poland's grain production, however, fed much of Europe.

King Jan III Sobieski, the Polish savior of Vienna in 1683, won many battles. But he was less successful trying to strengthen royal power against the nobles.

Central and Eastern Europe

The main powers in this region in about 1600 were the Habsburg emperors and Poland, which were later joined by Sweden with its Baltic empire. In addition, the Ottoman Turks ruled much of eastern Europe, as well as the Middle East and North Africa, and still they threatened to expand westward, attacking Vienna in 1683.

Lithuania

The Grand Duchy of Lithuania covered a much larger area than the present-day republic. It had been linked with Poland since the Middle Ages and in 1569 the two were formally united as a single state under the Polish king (who was also the grand duke of Lithuania). Poland became the largest state in Europe, stretching from the Baltic Sea to the Crimea, and it gained direct access to the sea.

Royal headdress belonging to King Jan III Sobieski of Poland.

THE OTTOMAN TURKS IN EUROPE

RUSSIA

PRUSSIA

POLAND-LITHUANIA

BUDA 1686

HOLY ROMAN EMPIRE • VIENNA 1683

AUSTRIAN EMPIRE

FRANCE

ST GOTTHARD 1644

STANILASTI 1711

VENICE

MOHÁCS 1687

PETERWARDEIN 1716 • BELGRADE

BLACK SEA

TUSCANY

NISH 1689 •

VARNA

OTTOMAN EMPIRE

ISTANBUL

REPUBLIC OF NAPLES

CORFU 1716 •

DARDANELLES 1656

CORINTH 1715 •

• CHESMÉ 1770

NORTH AFRICA

CORON 1685 •

CANDIA 1669

MEDITERRANEAN SEA

The Ottoman Provinces

The Muslim Ottoman Turks were more tolerant of Christians and Jews than Christians were of Muslims. Provinces such as Transylvania, Moldavia, and Walachia were practically independent, as long as they paid their taxes. Some of these territories were surrendered to the Austrian emperor and his allies in 1699.

To Austria in 1783

Venetian lands in 1783

Habsburg lands in 1640

Ottoman gains that were later lost

Ottoman lands in 1640

CANDIA 1669 — Major Ottoman battle, with date

The Ottoman Empire

During the 16th century, the Ottoman empire was one of the great powers of Europe. The empire flourished thanks to its control of major trade routes in the Mediterranean and East Asia. By 1640, Ottoman territories stretched from lands in Mesopotamia (modern Iraq) and parts of the Arabian peninsula in the east, to Algiers on the northern coast of Africa in the west. The Ottoman armies posed a constant threat to European borders.

Although the Ottomans suffered a huge naval defeat with heavy losses of ships and men at Lepanto in 1571, they were able to rebuild their fleet quickly.

During the time of the Polish-Lithuanian Commonwealth, an assembly of Polish nobles, called the Sejm, had the power to elect the king.

CENTRAL AND EASTERN EUROPE

1571
At the Battle of Lepanto (off the west coast of Greece), western European forces, led by Genoese and Venetian fleets, manage to halt the Ottoman advance.

1609
Under the Ottoman sultan Ahmed I (reigned 1603–1617) Istanbul's famous Blue mosque is built and the Kaaba sanctuary in Mecca is restored.

1617
Ottomans agree that the sultan's eldest son should succeed him as Mustafa I.

1619
Bethlen Gábor invades Hungary.

1655
Russians capture Vilnius.

1656
The first of the Köprülü grand viziers is appointed.

1664
Defeat at St. Gotthard begins Ottoman decline.

1684
Pope Innocent XI (1611–1689) organizes Holy League against the Ottoman Turks.

1699
Treaty of Karlowitz ends the war against the Ottomans.

The Ottoman Decline

By the beginning of the 17th century, Ottoman power was weakening as a result of poor government and economic difficulties. Many government posts were inherited rather than given according to merit, resulting in both inefficiency and corruption. There was a dislike of change, and the need for reforms was ignored. The Turkish cavalry were slow to adopt guns, and the navy was smashed at Lepanto. However, the Köprülü family, which held the post of grand vizier (Ottoman ruler) from 1656 to 1702, temporarily halted the decline.

Sultan Mustafa II (reigned 1695–1703) was forced to surrender large territories to Austria and its allies at the Treaty of Karlowitz in 1699.

Kara Mustafa Pasha, the grand vizier in 1676–1683, rode on this splendid Turkish saddle at the siege of Vienna.

Bethlen Gábor (reigned 1613–1629) was a Protestant ruler of Transylvania under the Ottomans. He invaded Hungary on his own accord and was elected king, but gave up the crown in exchange for toleration of Protestants in Habsburg Hungary.

Russia

The Grand Duke Ivan IV of Muscovy (1530–1584) became tsar (emperor) of Russia in 1547. This brutal ruler is known as Ivan the Terrible because he killed opponents, made more peasants into serfs (slaves), and expanded his kingdom. After a period of unrest, the Romanov dynasty came to power, and in the 1700s Russia finally became one of the major European states.

The Early Romanovs

The period after 1584, and especially after the reign of Tsar Boris Godunov (1598–1605) is known as the Time of Troubles. It was a period of famine, riots, civil war, rivalry for the throne, and Polish invasion. It lasted until Michael I became tsar in 1613. This was the start of the Romanov dynasty. Under Michael and his successor, Alexis (reigned 1645–1676), most peasants were forced into serfdom, various subject peoples, such as the Cossacks, rebelled, and the Orthodox Church split into two factions.

Portrait of Feodor III. During his short reign, from 1676 to 1682, thieves were deported to Siberia instead of having their hand and feet cut off, which had been the usual terrible punishment until then.

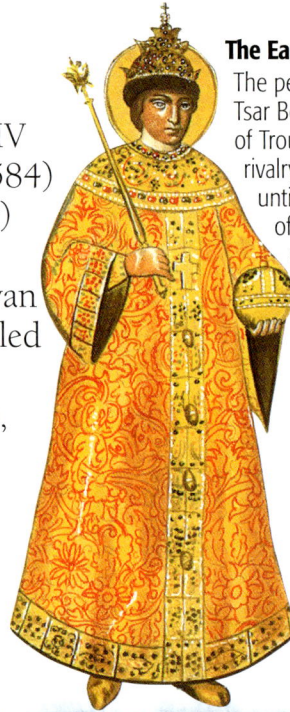

Russian Expansion

Russian territory expanded in the 17th century. It reached into Siberia, which was mostly barren but had a valuable product–furs. The pioneers there were the Cossacks (horsemen from the southern steppes), who first reached the Pacific coast. In the west, Russian influence increased when Poland surrendered the Ukraine. Most western Europeans still knew nothing about Russia, but contacts with it were gradually increasing.

The Cossacks were bands of adventurers and escaped serfs who were generally loyal to the tsar but hard to control and often rebellious. They settled the lands of Siberia, where the many river systems made the region navigable in the warmer seasons and also facilitated trade.

A decorative helmet made for Michael I, who was a great-nephew of Ivan the Terrible.

Russian architecture followed the northern European tradition of wooden buildings, and is famous for its towers and onion-shaped domes. This church in Moscow, begun in about 1693, reflects Russian and Orthodox styles, but it also has a touch of a new influence—the European Baroque.

Peter the Great

Peter I became sole ruler of Russia, aged 17, in 1689. He ruled until 1725. Supported by his own chosen friends, he was determined to modernise his backward country. His methods were sometimes violent and cruel—but they worked. He replaced the selfish boyars, Russia's former rulers, with his own men, and he brought western experts to Russia as teachers.

Peter I was the "father" of modern Russia. A gigantic personality, and over 6.5 feet (2 m) tall, he was an eager reformer, and even personally cut off the old-fashioned beards of some boyars (nobles).

LATE 17TH-CENTURY RUSSIA

SWEDEN
STOCKHOLM
WARSAW
ARCTIC OCEAN
ST PETERSBURG
RIGA
ARCHANGEL
MOSCOW
KIEV
RUSSIA
SIBERIA
OKHOTSK
YAKUTSK
BLACK SEA
TOBOLSK
TARA
YENISEISK
TOMSK
KRAZNOYARSK
KUZNETSK
NERCHINSK
CASPIAN SEA
IRKUTSK
JAPAN
CHINESE EMPIRE

The Church

After the Turks conquered the Byzantine empire, the Russian tsars regarded themselves as successors to the Byzantine emperors. Russia also became the chief home of the (Greek) Orthodox Church, which had split from Roman Catholicism in the 11th century. Byzantium influenced many Russian customs and culture, including art and architecture.

The Russian Empire

Peter founded a modern new capital, St. Petersburg, on the Baltic Sea. He referred to it as his "window on the west" because it faced western Europe. He also created a Russian navy. After victory over the Turks, Peter gained control of the Sea of Azov, and won access to the Black Sea. In a later war, he gained territory from Persia. His victory over the Swedes at Poltava in 1709 ended Swedish domination in the north and made Russia a great power at last.

Russia in 1551	Temporary expansion to 1600	Temporary expansion to 1600
Expansion to 1600	Losses by 1600	Losses by 1700

A medal struck to commemorate the founding of St. Petersburg in 1703.

Warfare and Diplomacy

Most sensible people in the 17th century believed war was cruel and wasteful, but they were also convinced that it was a natural part of life and so could not be prevented. Warfare was changing fast, mainly as a result of the improvement in guns, which led to many changes in military strategy and tactics. International relations and international law also developed at this time, but unfortunately this was not enough to prevent new wars.

Guns and Artillery

Guns improved so much that the flintlock muskets invented in the 17th century were still being made 200 years later. The great Swedish commanders preferred light field artillery and used nothing over 12 pounds (5 kg). They often massed their guns into groups called batteries, producing concentrated fire. Artillery became an organized unit of the army, and Louis XIV founded schools of artillery in France.

Professional Armies

Once, all soldiers were part-time, but by the 17th century most countries had well-trained professional armies—although work still existed for paid mercenaries. Leaders such as the Dutch Maurice of Nassau and the Swedish kings Gustavus II Adolphus and Charles XII introduced new, successful strategies. The day of the mounted knight-in-armor had passed. Cavalry was still important, but it became lighter and more mobile and acted in support of the infantry. Armed with pikes and muskets, the infantry was now the main fighting force.

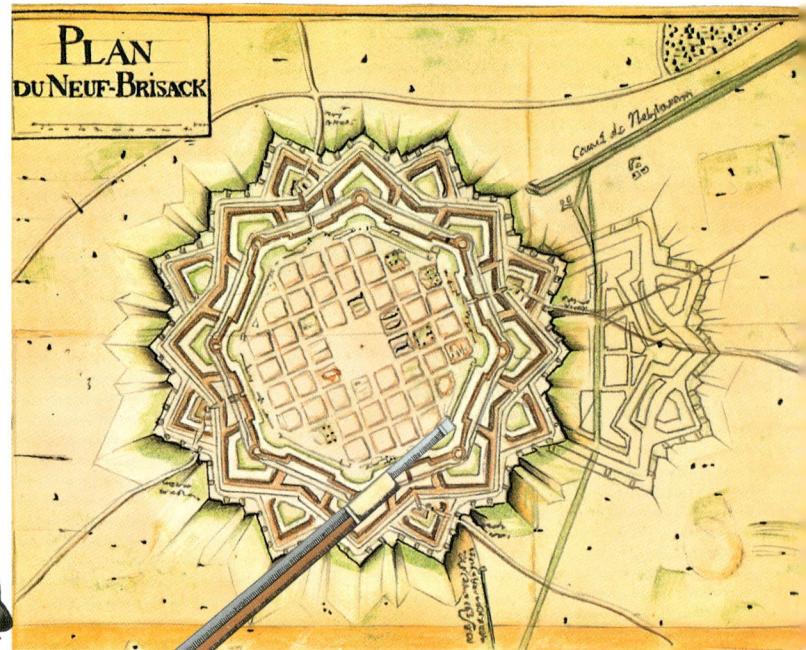

Vauban's plan for the fortified city of Neuf-Brisack, on the French side of the Rhine River. The walls are low, thick, and angled to divert cannon balls.

Siege Warfare

Sieges of towns or strong points were as important as open battles. Cannon had made Medieval castles obsolete, but strong fortifications designed to resist artillery fire were built on frontiers (especially the France-Netherlands border). They were designed by skilled engineers, such as the Frenchman, de Vauban (1633–1707), and were manned by large, permanent garrisons.

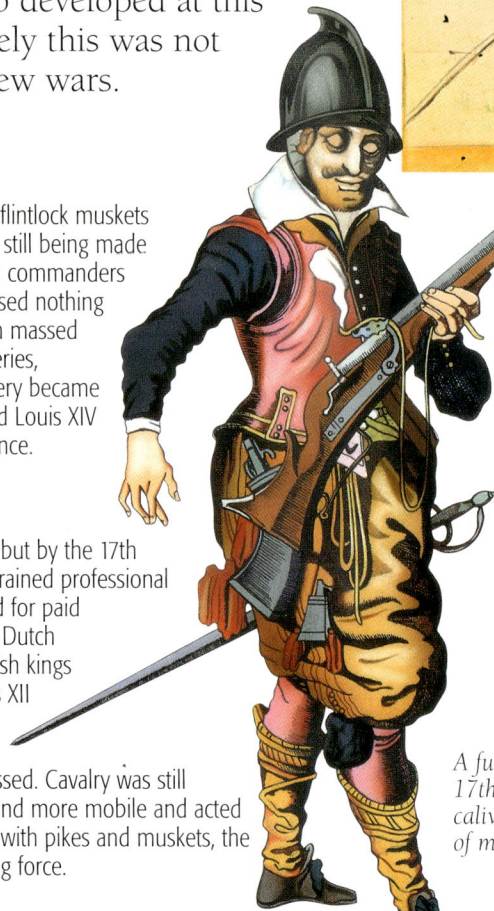

A fully equipped 17th-century German caliverman (a type of musketeer).

Soldiers of the Austrian royal army inserted their lances into a long wooden bar for better defence.

In the 17th century, arms became lighter and easier to manage, and also less affected by weather conditions.

The Effects of War

Ordinary civilians probably suffered most in times of war, often from their supposed defenders. Discipline was improving in some armies, the Dutch especially, but unpaid troops had to live off the land, which meant plundering, raping, and killing. War was also expensive. Even the rich treasury of Louis XIV of France was emptied by the cost of his many campaigns.

Diplomacy

Countries had peaceful relations, too. The beginnings of diplomacy can be seen in the rules of behavior drawn up for ambassadors sent to Medieval Italian states. The first permanent ambassadors were appointed in the 1400s, and rulers themselves sometimes met to discuss matters as well. In the 16th and 17th centuries, scholars such as the Dutchman Hugo Grotius (1583–1645) defined the privileges of ambassadors, which later became international law.

Two monarchs, Louis XIV of France (center left) and Philip IV of Spain (center right), meet on neutral ground to discuss matters of international concern.

WARS AND REVOLTS IN EUROPE DURING THE 17TH CENTURY

Political and Social Unrest

Many historians have described the 17th century as a period of revolutions in which political crisis was widespread in Europe. Although the causes of war and revolts differed from country to country, some scholars believe that an overall social crisis, marked by famines and plague, led to political unrest and popular rebellions.

- ● Center of political revolt
- ○ Center of popular revolt
- ▮ Popular revolt
- --- Political revolt
- ▮ War

Glossary

Absolute monarchy A system of rule in which the monarch has unrestricted power over his or her people. Absolute monarchs may claim to be accountable to God alone.

Agriculture Using land to grow crops and raise livestock.

Ambassador Someone who goes abroad to represent the interests of a ruler or government at a foreign court or government.

Architecture The art of designing and then supervising the construction of buildings.

Aristocracy A small group of people in society who inherited land, power, and privilege.

Artillery Large guns pulled by horses, or the branch of an army that uses this type of gun.

Assassinate To murder a ruler or important person for political or religious reasons.

Astronomy The science of studying the Sun, Moon, stars, and other heavenly bodies.

Cavalry The branch of an army made up of soldiers mounted on horseback.

Censorship When a government controls what may be printed in books or newspapers, and removes information that it does not want to be made public.

Civil war Armed conflict between different groups of people in the same country.

Colony A country's overseas land or territory.

Corrupt When someone behaves in a dishonest way in return for money or a gift.

Court The place where a monarch or ruler lives, including the buildings as well as all the courtiers (the other people who live there).

Devout To be very religious.

Diplomacy The art of managing international relations with other countries through negotiation rather than by warfare.

Dynasty A line of rulers coming from the same family, or a period during which they reign.

Edict A type of order or law passed by a ruler or government.

Empire All of the land controlled by a ruler or government, including overseas territories.

Economy The wealth and resources of a country or a region.

Execute To carry out a sentence of death on someone, usually as punishment for a crime or for political or religious reasons.

Famine When there is a massive shortage of food so that many people die of starvation.

Gable On a building, the triangular-shaped top part of a wall at the end of a roof.

Gilded Adorned with gold leaf.

Heir The next in line to the throne, who will become ruler when the current ruler dies or decides to abdicate (abandon the title).

Infantry The branch of an army made up of foot soldiers.

Mercenary A professional soldier available for hire, who fights for different armies in return for payment.

Minister An important official who serves a ruler or in a government.

Mint To make a coin by stamping a piece of metal.

Missionary A person who is sent on a religious mission to promote Christianity or a particular type of Christian belief.

Monarchy A country in which the ruler is a monarch who rules by his or her birthright.

Noble A high-ranking person who is a member of the aristocracy. They may be noble by birth, or may be awarded their title.

Obsolete Something that is out of date or old fashioned and has been replaced by something better and more advanced.

Parliament A formal gathering of people that debates and makes a country's laws. Members of parliament may be chosen by an election.

Peasant A member of one of the lowest classes of people, who earns his or her living through farming.

Philosophy The study of human thought about the meaning of life and the correct way to live.

Policy The course of action decided by a ruler, minister, government, or parliament.

Rebel To rise up and challenge a ruler or government, sometimes by force; also the name for a person who does this.

Reform To change an organization or system to make it work better or more efficiently.

Regent Someone who governs on behalf of a young prince or princess who inherits the throne before they are old enough officially to become the next monarch.

Republic A country in which the ruler, such as the Stadtholder in the Netherlands, is elected and is not a monarch who rules by birthright.

Revoke To cancel an official agreement, such as a law, edict, or treaty.

Secular Something that is not religious, for example a government, country, organization, festival, or building.

Serf A type of farm laborer, especially in Russia and eastern Europe, who belongs to a lord and has very little freedom.

Siege The surrounding of a city or fort by the army of their enemy in an attempt to capture it. A siege can last many days with the intention of starving the people inside so that they will surrender.

Tax Money people must pay to a government, church, or ruler to help support them or a particular cause.

Traitor A person who betrays someone else or an organization.

Treaty A written agreement between two or more countries or rulers, often drawn up to end a war.

Index